Darkness to Light

Finding Jesus in the Valley of Mental Illness

Compiled and Edited by Jessica Brodie

South Carolina United Methodist Advocate Press

Advocate Press

First published in the United States of America in 2023 by the South Carolina United Methodist Advocate Press.

Library of Congress Cataloging-in-Publication Data
Darkness to Light
p. cm.

Cover: Apriori1

ISBN 979-8-9883575-1-3

To all who struggle with often-invisible illness.
Please know you are seen, you matter,
and you are loved.

Table of Contents

†

Introduction

Mental and emotional health can be an arduous, exhausting marathon—and it certainly is in my home. One of our daughters has struggled for years with sometimes-debilitating anxiety and other issues, including depression. It's a massive challenge both for her and for me. I don't have anxiety or depression, so I've had to learn a great deal of compassion, patience, and flexibility over the years, as well as much about what it means as a Christian to love and care for someone with mental illness.

I'm no stranger to these issues. It runs in my family, and several relatives have been diagnosed with mental health disorders.

Still, walking through it day after day with my own child has helped me see things in a new light. In many ways, it's become my own struggle, and I'd gladly stand in my daughter's place, taking on her suffering as my own.

But God is calling me to a different purpose in the mental illness and mental health realm: that of an advocate and an ally, a voice to the sometimes voiceless.

Mental illness statistics are alarming, and the National Institute on Mental Health estimates more than one in five U.S. adults were living with a mental illness in 2021—that's nearly fifty-eight million people.

According to the National Institutes of Health, globally, nearly 15 percent of young people ages ten to nineteen experience a mental health disorder.

Numbers are even worse since the COVID-19 pandemic, and many say we are facing an unprecedented mental health crisis. The suicide rate is climbing, and availability of counselors, psychiatric care, and other resources is in woefully short supply. Many insurance plans don't even cover mental health care.

But there is one bright spot: More people are becoming increasingly vocal about mental and emotional health. While in the past there was a great stigma around these issues, and many people avoided dialogue out of embarrassment or shame, now society is embracing much-needed awareness about mental illness. We're discovering what many have known for years: that mental illness isn't someone's fault or caused by lack of faith or perspective. It's a genuine disorder, a brain malfunction often caused by genetic issues they can't possibly control.

Medication is seen in a new light, also. Just like people battling diabetes are helped with insulin, or cancer with chemotherapy and radiation, people with many mental illnesses often are helped by medication and therapy.

Counseling and other therapy are also becoming destigmatized as more people express their own mental health challenges.

As a Christian, I feel strongly that the church can be a resource and a support system for people with mental illness. I've known so many people who have reached their lowest, lost all hope, only to realize Jesus was right beside them the whole time.

Many of today's churches offer counseling, Stephen Ministry partners, support groups, and more. Others, by introducing people to Jesus and prioritizing discipleship, have been a pathway toward mental, emotional, and spiritual wellness.

The fourteen stories in this slim book offer a look at the personal mental health journeys of a number of people, sharing in many cases how faith played a major role in their healing journey. My own daughter, Avery, shares her story in "My Journey Back to Jesus," found on Page 25.

Whether you are struggling with your own mental and emotional health or you are supporting someone who is, I hope these stories offer hope and inspiration in what can be a dark, dark world.

Together, we can journey from darkness to light … the light of Christ.

—Jessica Brodie, editor
September 2023

1

Finding Hope in God

By Kelly Black

My depression started when I was in the fifth grade. I had a very hard teacher that year and didn't have any close friends around me at the time. Through that, I started to feel lonelier and more anxious, which was causing me to really struggle in school and at home. The overwhelming feeling over me was foggy and dark. I would spend hours alone, locking myself in the closet, just crying. I had the feeling of not wanting to wake up again the next day. Panic attacks came in the night, and I often cried uncontrollably. I wanted the misery to end.

It got to the point that I was crying so hard every morning, begging my parents not to take me to school. They decided it would be best for me to do home-schooling for the second half of fifth grade. Thankfully, my parents were supportive and caring enough that they allowed for this and took me to get professional help. It was at this time that I started on medication.

Through time, with the alleviation of stress and eventual effects of the medication, I began feeling better and suffering less from the extreme symptoms of depression I'd been feeling before. The psychiatrist expressed concern that public middle school the next year might cause more stress than I needed, and again, thankfully, I had the opportunity to attend a private Christian school nearby.

For maybe a year leading up to and during my sixth-grade year, I would listen to the song "Only Grace," by Matthew West, as I lay down to go to sleep. Through the new, relative stability in my life at this time, I was beginning to experience some of the relief found in the power of the Holy Spirit and in learning God's truth for my life outside of a depressed existence. That was the first time in my life I was really praying to God for his help and relying on him to help me with what I was going through.

During middle school, I started to make new friends. They were good influences, and I am now much more thankful for those influences than I knew I was at that time. The biggest blessing was a new neighbor and classmate, Anna, who had just moved in down the road. Even with great friends, there were still times I felt numb or anxious. I would become embarrassed if I had to take my medication during a sleepover. It was a struggle as a middle schooler to explain what it was and why I needed it.

Not all friends struggled to understand, though. There were others who had similar struggles, and we could talk in a way that we understood one another. Unfortunately, through those conversations, I became exposed to the idea of self-harm. This was not something I had encountered before, or even considered, but I came to know about it when a friend told me she was hurting herself. I would plead, "Don't do that to yourself!" But then at times would find myself doing it, too. For whatever reason, I felt like I needed to punish myself. This is something I still struggle with today, but there is hope.

My hope, and the biggest thing that helps me, comes

from knowing God has taken all of my feelings of guilt and shame away. He is in control, and he has good things in store for me as his child. All of the punishment needed to atone for my own shortcomings was carried out on the cross of Jesus Christ.

Throughout my teen years and into my twenties, I became more comfortable sharing my story and being honest with people I trusted about the struggles I'd had and continue to have. As I had more of those conversations, I found that others had a lot of the same struggles, or at least knew someone who had. It's been through my faith in God that I felt compelled to humble myself, to be openly weak, and to allow my struggles to be transformed into a tool to renew others and point to his sovereignty and grace over us.

During my twenties, just as my life seemed to be trending in a more positive direction—my mental health was largely stable, I was in a healthy relationship, and I had a pretty clear view of my professional growth goals—I went through a fair degree of trauma in my family. All were circumstances I never could've seen coming, and none I'd directly contributed to in any way.

My parents suddenly got divorced. We found out that my sister and her husband were abusing substances and were addicted. I had learned to take care of myself through my own mental health struggles, but these were certainly new challenges. There was very little I could do to make these things better. Sometimes all I could do was trust and pray.

Fortunately, I'd already come to know the importance of community and good influences in my life, and I knew my relationship with and dependence on God was possibly going to be the only thing I'd have to get me through. For that, again, I am thankful. My mental health challenges as a younger person had made me uniquely tough because I knew I needed to give it all to God. Today, he has redeemed all of what seemed to be so wildly out of control during that period of my life. My sister and husband are now sober and using their redemption stories to help others.

I am now a Certified Peer Support Specialist and volunteer facilitator with a church-based peer-led mental health support group called Fresh Hope. I get amazing opportunities to share my story about my mental health struggles and challenging experiences to empower people—and hopefully reveal to them the power that God has to carry us through and redeem all things. I also work with students in my job and get to build and maintain relationships with them, helping them to understand their identity and purpose.

I am thankful my path has led me to the place I am today, and God has blessed me. I choose to maintain an attitude of hope and gratitude every day, despite my circumstances, because God loves me. And God has proven his love by sending his one and only son, Jesus.

"May the God of hope fill you with all joy and peace as you trust in him, so that you may overflow with hope by the power of the Holy Spirit."—Romans 15:13

Black is a member of Advent United Methodist Church in Simpsonville, South Carolina.

2

A Conduit for Change

By Bill Barnier

I've been an unwilling victim of mental health trouble most of my life—collateral damage, as it turns out. Of course, we all have periods of personal stress, depression, or internal conflict. I view these as parts of life that bring opportunities to learn, to gather wisdom if you like. But I've been impacted directly by family, spouses, and close friends who have had the misfortune of being tormented by mental health issues caused by the actions of others.

There are organic causes of mental health issues, such as internal chemistry, hereditary traits, environmental impacts, nutrition, disease, etc. Event trauma is a separate cause. With modern advances in science and medicine, these causes can generally be identified and the results managed, reducing or eliminating the mental health issue.

Those with whom I've been involved were victims of mental and emotional issues as the result of actions by others. Those who became victims of horrific acts of physical violence, emotional abuse, and control were so profoundly affected they repressed the events so they could function. Those who could not turned to self-destructive behaviors, drugs, and alcohol, often leading to marital failure, job loss, accidental death, or intentional suicide. While there may be an underlying organic or inherited predisposition for depression or anxiety, often these are traits recognized by offenders and used against their victims.

For example: A young wife was becoming unsure if the marriage she was in was really what she wanted. She was not accepted by his stepmother, and she felt unwanted. After four years of struggle, with both working full time and saving for a house, they achieved their goal. But the enjoyment faded quickly when he had to take a better job working shifts more than sixty miles away. While she was at a decision point about their future, she became pregnant. Only a few weeks passed when complications forced a surgical intervention to save her life at the cost of the child and part of her reproductive system. She became angry, blaming him for her misfortune and unhappiness. Counseling could not solve her anger or resentment, and they divorced. She continued therapy for nearly two years, and contact faded away.

The former husband soon found another woman who seemed compatible with him, and they married. The couple was happy together with good jobs, a new home, and families who loved them. But the wife was unable to fully function in the bedroom. Though he was loving and patient, after three years it was becoming obvious there was a deeply rooted problem. Physical exams revealed no issues, so a mental health professional was the next step. After months of therapy the problem was unresolved, and divorce ended the relationship.

Finally, after two years of intense therapy, hypnosis, and supervised chemical therapy, it was revealed that the woman had been sexually abused by her grandfather, beginning at about age two and continuing for an estimated five years. It was also revealed that the grandfather had molested his own daughter for years with the full knowledge of the grandmother. Neither mother nor daughter ever functioned normally and neither wanted to endure the pain and embarrassment of prosecuting the eighty-five-year-old abuser. He died hated and lonely, his victims deprived of normal lives.

The surviving husband, twice divorced, remained single for eight years. He worked and traveled in foreign countries, then moved to a different state to start a new business. He became involved with a woman who hid her alcohol abuse very well, though her two teenage daughters knew the whole story and said nothing. Moving in together finally brought out the truth and a marriage plan, and the relationship ended. When she was forced to vacate their home because of her refusal to seek help, she attempted suicide.

At about the same time, an unplanned meeting as part of his volunteer service placed him in direct contact with a local government employee who was lovely, appeared very professional, interested in him, and let him know it. She was recently divorced, with two children under joint custody and successfully assisting a multimillion-dollar, multiagency public service department. Because she was not able to meet her financial needs, they decided to share living expenses. After a year passed, she forced the marriage issue, and he agreed. He had some knowledge of her past, but not the severity or the steps her former husband would take to deny her any happiness or a healthy relationship with her children.

Not long after the wedding, problems arose from her abusive parent, her former husband, her abusive boss, and her brainwashed daughter that began an exceptionally long list of financial, legal, and employment problems for them. There was a long line of users and abusers in her life who had found her as an infant and contained her in their sphere of direct influence for more than thirty years. In hindsight, it can be surmised from photographs and childhood stories that she was probably born with hereditary depression, compounded by abusive and irresponsible alcoholic parents living in an unhealthy situation.

Raised in the deep South in the sixties in an environment of male domination, justified by Southern Baptist ideology, her life path was controlled, and she was not allowed to venture out of their control or question anything. She was never permitted to live in the world outside of her mother's influence, was not allowed to grow emotionally, and was given to another abuser of the same kind in marriage. While keeping a home and trying to raise two small children, she was forced to take a job under the control of another tyrant abuser. After another five years of enduring all manner of physical and psychological abuse, she decided she would take her husband's life, then her own. Only a last moment of clarity prevented the potential crime, and she left the home and her children to save her sanity.

For brevity, let me say the influence those people had in her life was probably criminal. Her boss continued his control and abusive behavior, and her former husband continued his revenge with harassment, legal and financial troubles, and ruining her relationship with her children with vindictive lies. Several attempts at therapy were unsuccessful.

After eighteen years of exceptional work—which garnered praise from local and state agencies and awards from as far as the Pentagon—she became unable to do her work and was forced to retire on disability. Guilt became a blanket over her soul because guilt was a primary tool used by her abusers. Her new husband supported her and became her only island of sanity. Her daughter abandoned their relationship and her son did not, though the manner and attitude he learned from his father still influences their relationship.

Medical professionals and mental health practitioners are overwhelmed and are often ill-equipped to do much more than try this pill or that pill. They listen to the patient but often forget them as soon as they leave the office. Monthly appointments are only a bandage over a psychotic wound that sometimes takes a lifetime to create.

In this case, the elements of disaster came together. Depression, anxiety, a pharmaceutical "salad," alcohol, a loss of self-worth, guilt, physical manifestations, and behavioral elements met irresponsible medical advice to abruptly stop a depression medication without a replacement. The result was an attempted murder/suicide, which only God Almighty was able to stop without law enforcement action.

The remainder of this story would take several pages to convey. But suffice it to say that the outcome was positive. There were professionals who did interrupt the destructive course. Perhaps the most influential, however, was the love and support they received from their Methodist pastor. God was given full control, and through him, the fear of judgment was calmed. God's grace brought the couple to him for peace.

The people who have come into their lives are supportive and offer alternatives to the too-common path of destruction. They are rare, to be certain. And they continue to be sent by God at the time and place they are needed. Though her lifetime abuse left not one visible external mark, the internal physical damages derived from stress are permanent.

Their relationship is different, but they now understand that God has a plan for both. They're finally listening.

One could argue that the loving husband in these cases is predestined to be attracted to troubled mates. The cumulative effect on him over a lifetime succession of abused spouses and companions has also placed him as an abuse victim. In each case, he was a conduit for change while sacrificing a large segment of his life. Though not acknowledged until later years, his faith in God and his commitment to honor his promises to these women were instrumental in saving lives destined for self-destruction.

But make no mistake: the toll of emotional abuse and the results of the hidden stress for victims and those around them are potentially deadly.

As our human species evolves away from core spiritual values and becomes greedier and more self-centered, the stresses of our world become unmanageable, even for the strongest among us.

Spirit soldiers grow weary of offering pathways to peace and mental stability to those who no longer know how or are unwilling to listen.

Barnier is a member of St. Paul's Methodist Church, Ridgeland.

3

Caution: Objects in Mirror are Closer than They Appear

By David Bryant

On May 25, 1996, my briefcase contained an impressive resume of two bachelor's degrees and two master's degrees. I had a successful career with significant accomplishments and a secure future, living in a roomy house in an affluent neighborhood with a just-begun career change, a family, a wife, a son, and all the trappings of comfort and luxury.

Yet there, in pain and loneliness and self-pity, I lay in the crawl space under my house with a loaded gun and a bottle of vodka, no longer caring which killed me but resigned to that inevitable death, helpless and hopeless.

A neighbor opened that scuttle-hole and bravely brought me out. An out-of-town friend was called who asked me two questions: "Are you an alcoholic?" and "Are you willing to do anything to get sober?"

Upon my answers—"yes"— a stranger came, took me to an Alcoholics Anonymous meeting and, for the first time of many, I was able with relief and hope to say aloud, "My name is David, and I'm an alcoholic."

After that first step, I was lost. I realized I didn't understand "God as I understood him." I accepted a belief in

God and the Trinity, yet I had no relationship beyond an academic, intellectual understanding and a morbid acceptance of my own abjection: irredeemable.

I still didn't know.

I had studied, read, and searched through the Bible, commentaries, concordances, and self-help literature. I had conversations, debates, and arguments. I visited centers of different beliefs and denominations: churches, synagogues, cathedrals, monasteries, and places of quiet isolation.

But there was always only me … I still didn't know.

I began to get a glimpse as I realized that true humility and my purpose in life, which had evaded me all my life, was fairly straightforward: to seek God's will and be of service to my fellows. So far, so good.

Then, on page 53 of the chapter titled "We Agnostics" in the book *Alcoholics Anonymous*, third edition, I discovered two life-changing sentences: "When we became alcoholics, crushed by a self-imposed crisis we could not postpone or evade, we had to fearlessly face the proposition that either God is everything or else he is nothing. God either is or he isn't."

What was my choice to be? I reached back to the God of my childhood and recited the Lord's Prayer, the Apostle's Creed, and Psalm 23 as though my life depended on it—which, of course, it did.

Then I took the next steps.

Now, twenty-three years later, having lost family, friends, and a lifestyle, I have a new life—one of hope filled with happiness, joyousness, and freedom. A life with just enough adversity to show me my own powerlessness and reliance on God.

I know! I know that the intuitive knowledge of "that which used to baffle me" is the Holy Spirit within me. I know Jesus as a very real being to whom I can go for guidance and intervention, sitting at God the Father's side with his head often in his hands saying, "Yes! He is a struggling, failing, disobedient sinner, but he's my struggling, failing, disobedient sinner!"

I know Father God, who hears my petitions and silent groans, says, "I made you, I know you, I love you—in spite of yourself." I know a life with loved ones, friends, and family with whom I live, love, share, and grow ... warts and all.

I know!

When did this miraculous salvation occur? The only answer I can give is, "Somewhere along the way." Somewhere in not giving up, not giving in, stumbling, falling, and trying again. Somewhere in crying out in pain, laughing in joy, stepping out in fear, cowering in desperation, and realizing that God had done for me what I could never have done for myself and would, therefore, do it again. Somewhere in finding a life partner who leads, guides, nurtures, and loves as God's disciple of my heart. Somewhere in staying the course. Somehow I discovered the answer. I knew.

And now that I know, I can't not know. I am once again powerless but never again hopeless or helpless, for I am of God.

Now I take each step in faith—not that I will succeed, overcome, or prevail, but in the faith, trust, and belief in Jesus's words, "For I will always be with you."

So what have I learned through the experiences of eighty-nine-hundred-plus days of sobriety? I've learned that without conscious contact with God, I can and will fall back into every character defect that kept me drunk and separated me from the Son and more. I've learned that the culminating maintenance steps of the AA Twelve Steps are the embodiment of the intentional application of both the fruit of the Spirit and the spiritual gifts. Instead of pharisaic interpretation and justification of scriptural exclusion, I've learned I'm far more concerned with the Beatitudes, the remainder of the Sermon on the Mount, and the teachings of Jesus from his so-called trial by the Pharisees to his commands defining love to Peter.

I've learned that I am just as arrogantly and egoistically invested in my "rightness" and "righteousness" as are those against whom I rail, and oft times only the intervention of the Holy Spirit saves me from myself.

So how did I come to know Jesus? Slowly and surely. Down rabbit holes of doubt, anger, grief, and frustration. Through questioning and unbelief. In joy, celebration, hope, happiness, joyousness, and freedom.

I came to know Jesus "in spite of myself" through life's rearview mirror of willingness.

Caution: Objects in mirror are closer than they appear.

Bryant is a member of Bethesda United Methodist Church in Easley, South Carolina.

4

My Journey Back to Jesus

By Avery Connor

I still remember the first panic attack I had in public.
I was in third grade, and we had switched classrooms
for the day. We were learning about multiplication, and
math has always stressed me out. My nine-year-old brain
just couldn't wrap itself around all the complicated steps.
Within minutes, I could feel the room becoming smaller,
and it seemed like eyes were watching me.

My heart began to pound, and my cheeks grew hot. I
remember that it was the beginning of winter, right before
Christmas break. I was wearing heavy, fur-lined Ugg boots,
and I desperately wanted to take them off. I was trying to
stay calm, mostly because I was embarrassed about what
everyone else would think about me.

The girl sitting next to me noticed something was wrong
and asked if I was OK. I told her I was just feeling a little
sick to my stomach, but everything would be fine. However, I soon figured out everything would indeed not be fine.
I started to get dizzy, and my vision began to blur. I knew I
needed to tell my teacher.

She took one look at me and immediately sat me down
in a swivel chair. She wheeled me out of the room quickly.

On the way to the nurse's office, I noticed several students looking at me in the hallway. I could feel their eyes on my back, and that made me feel even worse. I started to hyperventilate. Eventually, the school sent me home, thinking I had a stomach bug. I thought so, too. I did have a stomachache, and I did feel clammy. But as time passed, that "stomach bug" didn't go away. I experienced this over and over again, and a visit to the nurse's office became a part of my daily routine.

When tests showed nothing was wrong physically, my mom took me to a counselor. Eventually, my problem was revealed. I was diagnosed with Generalized Anxiety Disorder. Those frequent stomachaches and dizzy spells turned out to be panic attacks, overthinking, mental battles, and much more. Between medication and counseling, I learned to cope and how to manage my anxiety.

But then, several years later, I entered middle school, and that's when my battle with depression began. Mean girls, social media, constant comparisons, and extreme mood swings played a huge role in my life. I began to feel exhausted, no matter how much sleep I'd had the night before. Depression medication and therapy helped, but it definitely didn't solve the problem.

When the COVID-19 pandemic hit, I was at an extreme low. I became isolated, and I stopped reaching out to most people. My room became my refuge, my favorite hiding place. I spent the majority of my time in bed, claiming to be sick. I did have some health problems, but what I didn't realize was that the depression was making everything worse. It eventually took control of my life.

I grew fascinated with death and thoughts of the afterlife. Darkness consumed me, and, although I'd been raised in the church and believed in God, I was in absolute despair. Often I would ask my mom heavy and morbid questions. Tragic news stories and true crime preoccupied my mind. I felt completely hopeless, and I told my mom almost daily that I would never get better, and that I didn't see a way out of the never-ending spiral my life had become.

Eventually, I begged God to "just take me." My pain was way too much to bear, and I was seeking relief from my misery. I experienced suicidal ideations, and it quickly became all I ever thought about. My days were filled with hopelessness, pain, and complete numbness. I felt dead inside, and although I didn't know it, the enemy convinced me I was alone and that no one else was going through this. Many of the people around me didn't understand my struggles, either. They took it personally and thought "tough love" would fix me. What they didn't realize is that tough love doesn't work with mental illness. I was in an extremely difficult and vulnerable time in my life, and others being harsh and demanding most certainly did not help.

However, I was unaware of one key thing: Jesus was with me every step of the way. He was with me through all of my pain and suffering. He was even by my side when I thought I had no hope left.

Over the next couple of years, I received excellent psychiatric care and high-quality counseling. I worked through my difficulties and learned how to cope in a healthy way. I talked with therapists, went to group counseling, and began work on Dialectical and Cognitive Behavioral Therapy (DBT and CBT). I tried a few different schools during this time, including a private Christian school, a large public high school, and a virtual charter school. While I was in a much better place, I was still struggling.

Ultimately I realized the missing piece was faith. It instantly clicked in my head. During my darkest season, I could feel myself stepping away from Jesus. I felt very isolated, and I tried to cope with worldly things: food, material possessions like new clothing and makeup, and movies and TV shows that helped me escape my problems. I thought there was something out in the world that would help me overcome my struggles. My brain was filled with thoughts such as, "If I only had this, everything would be better," and "Oh, this person has this thing, and they are so happy. I need to get that so I can be happy, too." I expected that getting the newest iPhone or buying those on-trend Nike sneakers would make me feel included and would help me fit in. But in reality, I wasn't happy. I was miserable, and nothing I tried to cope with changed my mental state. I was trying to work on my faith because my mom and certain people I followed on social media kept encouraging this. But it always felt so inauthentic and impersonal.

Then one day, it hit me: I needed to stop living like—and for—everyone else. I am not a part of the world. Instead, I am a part of God's kingdom, and I am a child of God.

After that, my prayer life got more personal. I started reading the Bible, and I realized I had been holding a big part of myself back from God and not being fully honest with him. I needed to start being real with him.

That is when my healing journey really, truly began.

Soon my mood began to improve significantly, and I started regularly attending church again. Now, I am doing so much better. I spend time in the Bible daily, and I work hard on my relationship with Jesus. I found that joy does not come from the world. True joy starts with the Lord, and we don't have to pretend to be perfect with God. He is here for us, he is with us, and he is in us.

Things will never be perfect. I am diagnosed with mental illness. But because of my faith, I am stronger, wiser, happier, and filled with the Holy Spirit. I have hope, and all is well with my soul.

Connor, a teen, is a member of Mount Horeb Church in Lexington, South Carolina.

5

A Journey Out of Darkness

By Penelope Wesley

It is a journey. It is a process.

The Bible tells us how the woman with the issue of blood suffered twelve years. She sought Jesus, believing if she could touch the fringe of his garment, she would be healed. This woman's story, found in Mark 5, tells how she had been isolated, withdrawn, and called unclean. She took a risk. She went to Jesus trying not to be noticed, but Jesus knew power had left him. He noticed her even though she was in a large crowd. Her physical illness was taboo in her culture, similar to how the world has viewed "mental illness" throughout the centuries.

Mental illness is more accepted today than when I was diagnosed in 1972 with Major Recurrent Depression and Post-Traumatic Stress Disorder. However, we have a long way to go. Most people who suffer from a mental illness have difficulty talking about it. Is it fear of not knowing what to say? What to do? Is it because at times we feel inadequate, flawed, or have a sense of shame and have trouble being real about who we are?

For healing to begin, steps must be taken to reach out for help, just as the woman in Mark 5 reached to touch the hem of Jesus's garment.

I will always carry the image of the day I reached out. I remember where I was standing and what I was doing. Feelings had overtaken my will. That was the day I surrendered my depression to God.

I was working at the cancer center. I was depressed again, lacking energy, getting by on little sleep, struggling to get to work, and fighting to concentrate. Standing behind the medication cart, I knew I couldn't go on. I was at the end of my rope and feeling nothing to hold on to. I desperately wanted someone to hear my cries. To know my pain. To help.

These feelings were not new. I'd been in this place before. Through the years, I'd experienced days consumed by episodes of cutting, overdosing, suicidal ideations, and attempts to end it all. I'd lived in violence, with verbal and emotional abuse, and had been a victim of sexual abuse. Why should I try or care?

That day my legs became weak. Grabbing the sides of the cart, I leaned across the top and held on, crying out to God. I will never forget my words.

"Lord, help me!" I prayed. "I want to be healed. I'm tired, weary. I can't keep going through this. I don't want to live this way. Oh, Lord, I need healing. Therapy and medication are not enough. I have struggled since childhood, dealing with it however I could. I am haunted by PTSD. I keep numbing the pain just to make it go away. Please, God, even if I don't work again as a nurse, I want to be healed. God, where else can I go? I'm tired of endless treatment, hospitalizations, living with all the anxiety, feeling unsafe, and not trusting anyone."

I remember questioning my thoughts and the words I had prayed. Did I really mean that? What would I do? But

I didn't care. I wanted God to set me free regardless of how long it took.

My prayer of surrender was powerful. But the endless struggle to put one foot in front of the other became harder. My dad was suffering in his own prison with Alzheimer's. After more than two years locked within the walls of the veteran's hospital, each day became a slow disconnect to himself, family, and life.

Then the day came when I was sitting on his hospital bed holding his hand. His last breath was shallow, with once-prolonged gaps between breaths now turned to silence. I stared, waiting for another breath, but there was none. I knew his struggle was over. Removing the oxygen tubing from his nose, I remembered how he'd hated anything touching his face. I lingered, staring at the man I once knew. Growing up, I'd witnessed a side of him I do not like to remember: a life of anger, alcoholism, and verbal, emotional, and spousal abuse. Now I knew he was at peace. He was not suffering, but the numbness I felt continued to haunt me.

I had to do something. After multiple hospital admissions and long periods of missing days of work, I resigned from nursing and stepped into the world of the disabled. Losing my home, I moved to my hometown to live with my mother and spent the first two years fighting for treatment and insurance, dealing with unpaid bills, and waiting for approval from Social Security.

One Sunday, sitting with my mother in my home church, the pastor's words grabbed my attention. I experienced God's word leaping off the page like a splash of cold water between my eyes. It was the story of the bleeding woman, from Mark 5:25-35. Her pursuit of healing. Her desperation after twelve years of aloneness, weariness, and weakness. Money exhausted. She knew her need and believed Jesus could heal if she could get close enough.

Jesus said to her, "Daughter, your faith has healed you. Go in peace and be freed from your suffering" (Mark 5:34).

I wanted that healing. I wanted that faith. I wanted to touch the hem of his garment. I wanted to hear him call me "Daughter."

So I prayed. I begged. Knowing I may only have the faith of a mustard seed, I clung to those words. Bent by the weight of depression, I had deep emotional wounds needing extensive healing by the Master's hand, a spirit of fear and years of bottled feelings and words never spoken.

That Sunday I began making my way toward the cross. For many years, a spirit of depression had consumed me. I often wandered in the wilderness, lost and weary. At times, searching was like being in a giant maze finding I had to turn around and try another way. I had struggled. I had wandered from God. My focus was not always on him but on my own selfish needs and the ways of the world. I struggled with those up and down feelings of hopelessness and despair. It was a very lonely place to be.

But God was with me in my journey out of darkness. He led me to a therapist and a doctor who worked with me. My attempts to verbalize my thoughts and feelings increased my silence and withdrawal. Over the years, this became my usual response when I felt threatened or anxious about talking. After months of struggling to reach me, my therapist discovered my ability to express my thoughts and feelings through writing. This became my way to connect with her. My progress was slow, but trust was gradually built.

God continued to guide me, knowing the right time and where I needed to be.

Christmas week 2010 I moved from Kentucky to South Carolina to be near my sister and her family. After a couple of years of searching and adjusting, I joined a United Methodist church where I felt accepted and, in time, found ways I could serve. I am grateful for a church family that believed in prayer and support. I am grateful for close friends who gave time, patience, and love, being there for me and allowing my trust to grow. I am grateful for my pastor who faithfully prayed and many times had the faith for both of us. He spent hours reading page after page of my writing, listening, guiding, encouraging, and trusting God to work. I will always be grateful to him.

But most of all I give God the glory. I rejoice as I am free from the triggers and nightmares from PTSD. I praise God for the healing of memories and the freedom I now feel. He mended my broken pieces, and I chose forgiveness. To me it is a miracle, one only he can do. I thank him that I am his daughter and know my peace comes from knowing he is present in every step of my journey, even when I am suffering.

I know now my diagnosis was made from several factors including environmental circumstances as well as a physical chemical imbalance. Depression seems to be my "thorn in the flesh" (2 Corinthians 12). I am grateful for the healing that has happened, but the chemical imbalance continues. I would like to say I am cured, but I can't say that yet. I am more aware of the symptoms and can say I am more accepting of it than in the past.

However, my depression looks different today. The duration and depth is less. My faith gives me strength, as I know when I suffer, God's light will come even in the darkness. I have learned better coping skills and turn to support when these times come.

I continue to pray for complete healing, but if not, I know God is with me.

As I reflect over my walk with the Lord, I remember a time as a twelve-year-old praying for God to change my father. I didn't need to wait for an answer. The Spirit of God gently said, "First, you must love him like he is." This was my first answered prayer in this manner. God revealed himself to me, and he was real.

God did answer my prayer in his own way and his own time. After I moved away from home and began working as a nurse, my dad attended a revival service. That night he responded to the altar call given by his nephew. He knew he needed God and asked for forgiveness and help. That night he walked away a new person, never to smoke or drink alcohol again. I have sweet memories of attending worship services with both parents, my siblings, and their families.

As I had to do with my dad, I realize accepting someone's behavior is not always easy. This includes accepting my own behavior. I made wrong choices and wallowed in my pain while struggling to let go of hurts caused by others. God was waiting, wanting me to feel his love. Out of fear of his judgment and expectations of perfection, I built walls. He seemed so far away.

It wasn't until after experiencing healing of damaged emotions, memories, and trauma that I would know the meaning of God's love and grace. It's a love that has shown me I am his daughter, and he is always near when I reach out to him on my journey.

Now a member of Liberty United Methodist Church in Liberty, Kentucky, Wesley moved from Bethesda United Methodist Church, Easley, South Carolina.

6

What God Gives

By the Rev. John Jordan

In the early 1980s, I worked at the Mental Health Clinic of Jacksonville, Florida, as a case manager with persistently mentally ill adults. One client, Emma,* had a long history of multiple hospitalizations at Northeast Florida State Hospital.

During one session, I asked Emma if she attended church. This was to assess her social support network, not to find out how religious she was.

Emma looked me dead in the eye and said, "John, let me tell you about church."

"OK," I replied.

She began, "I go to church. The preacher tells people to come to the front so he could heal them. I go to the front. The preacher lays hands on me and says I am healed. I go home and throw away all my medicine because I am healed.

"A few weeks later I end up in the state hospital.

"I get out and am watching television. The preacher on the television says to lay your hands on the TV and you will be healed! I lay my hands on the TV. I am healed! I throw away my medicine.

"A few weeks later I am back in the state hospital.

"I get out again. I am listening to the radio. A preacher comes on the radio and says to lay your hands on the radio and you will be healed. I lay my hands on the radio and I am healed! I throw away my medicine.

"A few weeks later I end up back in the state hospital."

Emma pointed at me and said, "John, after that, I realized God gave me this clinic and this medicine to make me well."

Emma learned to have faith in the means God was giving her to be well rather than what she thought would heal her. She had faith that her healing would come through the clinic and medications, not in some supernatural way.

*The name has been changed for privacy.

Jordan is an elder in the South Carolina Conference of The United Methodist Church.

7

When Heaven Came Down to Earth

By the Rev. John Culp

It was December 1988, and I was working on my sermon when the thought came to me to walk the grounds of the state hospital on Bull Street in Columbia. I wanted to give a special thanks to God for my dad's recovery and release from there when I was a twelve-year old child.

In the 1950s, there were no drugs for mental illness, and the state hospital was the only option. At that age I had been fearful of this place, yet my love for my father was great. Now, after thirty-one years, the time had come for me to walk these grounds again and give thanks to my heavenly Father. My father was given back to me and my family, and he overcame his depression. We all experienced a miracle of grace.

On December 8, 1988, I went into the Chapel of Hope there, which was built with the bricks from the wall that once surrounded the hospital. I had anxiety and uncertainty as I entered the chapel, as well as these feelings of the past.

My friend Tom Summers, the chaplain of the hospital, was in his office, and I was thankful he was because I needed a friend to share my story and feelings with at this holy moment. I realized that, in a spiritual way, we can journey in time to be with those we love and claim these relationships.

I shared my story and my father's life with my priest, Tom, and I asked him to join me in the chapel to give thanks and praise, as well as to be with my earthly father and my heavenly Father. There was music in the chapel, and I felt very close to God in that moment, as if heaven and earth came together (Ephesians 1:9-10). There was a deep cleansing of my soul and a deep release of feelings.

I am thankful for this gift to go back and reclaim this moment of grace in Dad's life and to be set free of the fears, misconceptions, and insecurities, as well as to realize the new hope and new love that is ours.

In this eternal moment, my dad and I shared a beautiful time of peace and spiritual freedom. I do believe that heaven came down to earth at Christmastime. My spiritual Christmas gift was given to me in being able to claim this miracle and be thankful to a loving God for giving my father back to our family and especially to me.

Our biblical friends were always taking their journeys, such as Mary and Joseph, and I believe we should take ours in a spiritual way at Christmas. Jesus invited his special friends into the garden with him, and now I invite you to share this special Christmas gift I received from Christ.

May we ponder in our hearts, minds, and souls as Mary did about the amazing stories of grace in our lives.

Culp is a retired elder in the South Carolina Conference of The United Methodist Church.

8

Mental Health and the Church

By the Rev. Sheera Yates

Mental health and the church begins with the pastor. It is imperative that the pastor recognizes wellness is not just a physical aspect but comes from a biopsychosocial spiritual approach personally and for the congregation.

The church is the one place where congregants can seek counseling care without stigmatization, especially in rural areas. Recognizing we have experienced challenges over the last couple of years, comfort and encouragement are sought to reduce disease related to stressful situations, traumas, crises, and the pandemics of COVID, social injustice, social inequalities, and disparities in health care, finance, housing, and education. Pastors, congregants, and the community are looking for relief. There is burnout experienced by caregivers and their families, along with pain associated with bereavement. There is a need to grieve and mourn.

Where do you turn? The negative connotation and stigma associated with mental health counseling caused me to ponder ways the church can make a difference. As a pastor of Franklin United Methodist Church, Denmark, South Carolina, I made a concerted effort to gain additional training in pastoral care and counseling including taking classes and seeking certification in a number of areas. These include mental health first aid for youth and adults; CPR/first aid; Our Journey of Hope Cancer Treatment Centers' program for pastors and congregations; domestic/intimate violence; stress, crisis, and trauma counseling: spiritual impact and implications; mindfulness in recovery; trauma-informed care; spiritually integrated psychotherapy; navigating gender dysphoria and gender diversity in a therapeutic setting; afrofuturism, afropessimism, and the Black church; womanist/feminist pastoral care; human trafficking; basic motivational interviewing; cognitive behavioral techniques, QPR Suicide Prevention Gatekeeper; Living Works Faith suicide prevention; and AS+K to Save A Life Gatekeeper leader training.

To assist others, it is imperative that I have a basic knowledge of social issues and my social location. I have to be willing to expose myself to other perspectives and be willing to compassionately listen, thoughtfully respond, and comfortably refer those to whom I am offering pastoral care. It is imperative that the pastor recognizes it involves others.

Understanding the mission and ministry of the church in serving, the Franklin church family initially started with Faith Activity and Nutrition (FAN) and has branched to include our version of Our Journey of Hope Ministry. We decided to not limit it to physical care and cancer patients but to help in any way we can serve, including suicide gatekeeper training, referrals, and volunteering. We want to be a safe space where people can come for spiritual encouragement, not feeling compelled to be immersed in scripture, but able to comfortably talk and become empowered. We want to meet people where they are. We do not profess to have all the answers but will seek them and refer as appropriate.

Communication is key. The art of conversation is one method of beginning. Our church members and community members have taken AS+K Suicide Prevention Gatekeeper training as a start. We have a diverse congregation with experience in many vocations. We are committed and begin with a positive attitude filled with gratitude. We are removing all negativity, anger, resentment, pity, pettiness, hurt, discouragement, and selfishness. We are forgiving as required by the Lord. We are loving while recognizing there are some things we may not like.

We recognize the difference between disappointment and discouragement. We are reflecting God's character of love, joy, peace, and contentment as intentional disciples seeking to fulfill his purpose, plan, and will for our lives as we serve as called. We uplift doing no harm, doing good, and loving God and others. We are becoming closer to God as we search and meditate on scripture, pray, encourage one another, and spend time with God.

We know our prayers are stimulated by faith, hope, and belief. We are reminded of our beliefs in our affirmation of faith in the Apostles' Creed Traditional Version. We are loving and serving. We are doing our best to eradicate behaviors that cause pain as we seek God's reconciling grace, mercy, favor, and restoration to his children, moving forward with forgiveness and reconciliation addressing concerns and promoting change.

May we live in the here and now, looking expectantly at the future.

Yates is a local pastor in the South Carolina Conference of The United Methodist Church.

9

Hope for a Better Future: Living with Bipolar Disorder

By Juliette*

My name is Juliette, and I live my life while having bipolar disorder.

It has been ten years since my first major manic episode, and I am now healthy and balanced. I have completed Dialectical Behavioral Therapy, and I take twelve pills every day. My doctor and I meet every three months to check in, and I meet with my therapist as needed. I am able to be a stay-at-home mom and wife as well as volunteer at church and in the local community.

The journey to this point was arduous and life-threatening, but I'm sharing it now as proof there is always hope for a better future.

To fully appreciate the complete shift that the manic, depressive, and mixed episodes had on my life, you must first understand who I was before this started. I graduated in the top five percent of my senior high school class while working after school and was student body president. I was voted Most Outstanding Leader. I was very active in our church youth group. In college, I worked three jobs and graduated with two degrees and a 3.0 average. I have always been driven, ambitious, and very much a perfectionist.

But there were always major and dangerous mood shifts I experienced that were normalized under the umbrella of hormones. From dangerous behavior during my teenage years to experiencing postpartum depression after my son was born, my bipolar diagnosis was normalized as responsive behavior to negative life events and blamed on my hormones.

I was twenty-six years old and newly divorced when I experienced my first manic episode, which was so severe no one could reach me or help me. At the time, my two-year-old son and I were living in a small duplex, barely making it on my salary as a quality assurance engineer at a software company. I had to pick up a second job at a makeup counter and was working a total of eighty to one hundred hours per week. My parents were watching my son more than I was seeing him on a regular basis so I could support us financially.

One day I snapped and became a person no one recognized, including me.

My "social life" began to take place late at night at bars with men I didn't know. I changed the way I did my make-up, wore wigs, and began to dress in a trendy and provocative way. Soon I sold my jewelry to get cash quickly and became very savvy at taking out quick-cash loans without thinking about the consequences. I slept with men I didn't know. I entered into meaningless relationships that I knew only I would benefit from. I started smoking. Over a five-month period, my son and I moved three different times because of the threat of eviction before we finally ended up at my parents' house. I eventually quit the makeup counter job and lost my quality assurance engineering job because of underperformance.

Then, I got a DUI after spending time with a man I didn't even know.

This was my rock bottom.

My parents were out of town with my son, and I had no one to call to help me. I spent the night in jail. I was alone, drunk, scared, and sick.

I was a divorced college graduate, voted Outstanding Leader in high school, had no job, was living at home, and now had a DUI. Nothing about the person I've described even resembled a Juliette anyone would have recognized. To everyone around me, including me, it appeared as though I was acting out because of the recent divorce. My actions could be—and were—explained away and normalized as postpartum depression and a recently failed marriage.

During the months it took to regain my driver's license and find a new job, I fell into a deep depression. It was so intense that it was hard for me to get out of bed and shower. To others, it appeared I had given up and simply didn't care. The truth was that I didn't have the energy to care. I simply wanted the pain to stop.

I could remember pieces of the manic episode that had turned my life upside down and didn't understand why I'd behaved in such a terrible way. Every moment of being awake was torture, and then dreams would haunt me while I slept. It was devastating and horribly embarrassing. I couldn't bear the memories. I would spend hours cutting my wrists so I could express the pain I felt so deeply. When I was caught doing that, I moved to my inner thigh. The guilt was crippling; I felt as though I couldn't breathe.

After a year, the fog finally lifted. I secured a position at a telecommunications company where I was respected and making decent money. My moods began to even out, and I began caring full-time for my son and paying off my debt. I now had insurance, so I went to a doctor who referred me to a psychiatrist. He listened to me and started me on simple anxiety medications.

Over the next four years, I was diagnosed with Major Depressive Disorder and General Anxiety Disorder and was on a treatment for both. During this time, I was promoted at work and remarried. My son, now six years old, and I moved from my parents' home to a neighboring county with my new husband to start our new life.

A year into our marriage, work became incredibly stressful. I had received another promotion and was doing well, but I couldn't handle the stress and experienced what is called a mixed episode. I began spending hordes of money again, drinking in excess, and abusing my anxiety medications. Little by little, I became a nonfunctioning member of our family. I was unable to stop the cycle on my own and began cutting my wrists and inner thighs again. I would write suicide notes—goodbye notes to my son.

I'm thankful to God my husband was committed to finding us help and answers.

Over a two-year period, I was admitted four different times to local behavioral health centers. It was there I learned about bipolar, anxiety, and depression disorders in depth. A new cocktail of medications was introduced. The attending psychiatrist told my husband about Dialectical Behavioral Therapy, DBT, and together they worked to get me on the waiting list to attend.

My DBT and Radically Open DBT lasted a total of three years. During this time I did not work but instead focused on therapy and finding the closest-to-perfect drug protocol that would balance my brain.

Even through my deep depression, my love for my son

and my husband never waned. The chemical imbalance causes behavioral changes but it does not stop love. Love, in many forms, is what propelled me forward to a better future.

We had many support systems during this time, including my family, our church family, my therapist, and my psychiatrist. My church family allowed me to continue to serve as a second Sunday school teacher while I was undergoing much of my therapy. I had my Mom's Growth Group and our church's mental health group to lean on. I was surrounded by cheerleaders who wanted me to succeed.

I believe it's important to put your feet where you want your heart to be. My heart wanted and needed to be in church. I was not an outcast but welcomed and given a place to serve during a very difficult time. I believe that service gave me a purpose when I needed one.

Currently, one of the most rewarding ways I am able to honor God is through Stephen Ministry, where I am a caregiver and actively listen to those experiencing difficult times. It is a way to make Bipolar Disorder, which is something ugly and devastating, so very beautiful.

I am now devoted to serving others in any way I can. I fully recognize that I have been given a second chance at life. My better future is now my present, and I am so thankful.

Juliette (a pseudonym) is a member of a United Methodist church in South Carolina.

10

Hearts for God Connect in a Special Way

By Linda Kidd

One of the saddest days of my life was late one afternoon as I was preparing dinner for my family. The telephone rang.

When I heard the message from the other end—that my sister had taken her life—I just began crying and screaming uncontrollably. Through all of her struggles, I never imagined it would come to this. Although I had spent many hours in my sister's home, sitting at her bedside, trying to help her get up and greet the day, it never seemed to be enough.

My sister was a very caring older sister. In our family of eight children, she was third and I was seventh. Some of my fondest childhood memories of her are eating the homemade fudge she would make for us or vacationing at Daytona Beach with her family. She always had a beautiful tan each summer. My memories of her are different from those of my older siblings, who experienced more strongly the struggles she had growing up. Looking back, they probably originated from a difficulty she sometimes experienced with self-esteem.

My sister married a good man, and they had two beautiful daughters. She sang in the church choir, helped with Sunday school, and was a wonderful cook, wife, and mother—on her good days. But when she was down, she was unable to get out of bed. She sought mental health counseling for her manic depression, and she always said her counselor told her she would attend counseling right up until they were about to get to the root of her problem. Then she would stop.

The feeling I had when I heard the news of my sister's death—that we can never do enough for our loved ones who struggle with mental illness—remained with me afterwards. In my heart, I vowed that one day I would find a way to reach out to help make a difference in the lives of those struggling with this terrible disease, to help heal their brokenness.

God opened the door to that opportunity some years later, in 2006. That is when a group of my fellow sisters in Christ at McCormick Methodist Church, in McCormick, South Carolina, came together to form the 24:7 Small Group. Initially, we were a Christ Care Group. Our church offered training to those interested in becoming Christ Care Group leaders, and I took the forty-hour course.

I had an ulterior motive for taking the course. I thought one of the other group leaders who took the course might want to focus on mental health, and I would join their group. That did not happen, however, so I saw this as a sign that God intended for me to form a group with myself as leader—a task for which I felt very inadequate.

Ten ladies joined me, and in 2007, our adventure began. We named our group the 24:7 Small Group. The name is derived from Jeremiah 24:7, "Then I will give them a heart to know me, that I am the Lord; and they shall be my people, and I will be their God, for they shall return to me with their whole heart."

We covenanted together to know God better through

biblical equipping, prayer, and living out Christ's love for one another and others. We used our collective gifts as a group to reach out with Christ's love to meet the needs of people outside the group. Through our group connectedness, I feel we help one another to live as Christ's disciples, working together to serve as Jesus served, to truly have "hearts for God" or "hearts of servants."

Of course, the mission emphasis for the group is mental health, and membership in the group is open to any who share an interest in mental health needs. The group sponsors regular luncheons, Bible studies, and events throughout the year at a mental health housing complex located in our town.

The complex houses twenty residents, and an average of eleven or twelve residents attend the events we sponsor in the community building. Each year, we prepare and share together five or six meals with our friends that also include fun activities like bingo and Bible studies. There is mutual sharing and growing in our faith as we learn from our friends, and hopefully they learn from us as well. Our faith has been made stronger as our friends share their faith with us. Each of the residents receives personal birthday cards from our group throughout the year, and we also remember them with Christmas gifts.

To our surprise, during Mental Health Awareness Month in May 2011, the 24:7 Small Group received a statewide award from Mental Health America of South Carolina when the group was named "Volunteer Group of the Year." A group of us traveled to Columbia to the MHASC Annual Meeting to receive the award.

It has now been sixteen years since we began our ministry, and throughout that time, 24:7 group members and our friends have laughed and cried together and reached out to one another as personal difficulties have occurred among us. Although 2020, the year of the pandemic, made it impossible for us to physically be with our friends, our group found creative ways to come together, observing social distancing and wearing masks as we reached out. Some of our members with compromised health situations were unable to join us physically, but they helped with contributions. It was very important to us that our friends knew they were not forgotten.

On my front porch, we bagged pandemic necessities—paper towels, toilet tissue, face masks, disinfectant supplies, hand sanitizers, rubber gloves, etc.—and sent them to our friends. On special occasions such as Valentine's Day and Halloween, we bagged pre-wrapped goodies and other items and sent to them with tags that read "You Are God's Favorite Valentine" and "Treats from Jesus." At Thanksgiving, we bagged meals of professionally prepared rotisserie chicken, canned goods, and pre-packaged foods for their Thanksgiving meal and sent these to them. At Christmas, we remembered them with gifts as we normally do.

It was important to us that our friends knew we were thinking of them, especially during the pandemic when they had to be isolated and alone.

Our group is thankful to God for his blessings that continue to provide us this opportunity to share his love with others. On a personal note, I thank him for the opportunity to honor in my heart the memory of my sister.

She was a beautiful Christian; I think she would be pleased.

Kidd is a member of McCormick Methodist Church, McCormick, South Carolina.

11

Christ, the Balm of Gilead

By the Rev. Elizabeth Sullivan

Several years ago I had an epiphany. It came after I asked myself a really strange question: What does the church have to offer that no other company or business has?

Well, the obvious Sunday school answer is Jesus. However, to the outsider, to the non-believer, that just doesn't really cut it. Of course, it is the absolute truth about what we as Christians have to offer the world, but it is not necessarily valued until one believes. So what do we have as the church that is so desperately needed by nonbelievers?

My epiphany came when I realized the answer to the question is something we share with each other often during Holy Communion:

Pastor to the People: In the name of Jesus Christ, you are forgiven.

People to the Pastor: In the name of Jesus Christ, you are forgiven.

We all need forgiveness. Don't we? As human beings, our greatest desire is to live in close loving relationships where we feel understood for who we are. Yes, it all sounds lovely, so ... what's the problem?

Well, the problem is that we are all broken and we all hurt

one another. And in order to live in long-lasting, meaningful relationships, we clearly have to learn how to both give and receive forgiveness. Bottom line, we are all sinners, and we need to receive forgiveness from God and from others and we also need to forgive others—and ourselves.

What the church offers to everyone is a deep understanding of what it means to forgive and to be forgiven. I don't say this lightly, because my faith is rooted in experiencing forgiveness and offering forgiveness.

It was winter 1991, and I was twenty-two years old and living in Cleveland, Ohio. I was in a cold and dark place in my life—physically, spiritually, and emotionally—so dark that, in fact, I was considering taking my own life. It was in this place of desperation, where I had tried everything else to make my own life work better, that I finally prayed and began to seek God in earnest. God showed up and answered my prayers.

I often wonder: Why God? Why me? Why did you speak to me so clearly, and why am I deserving of your salvation and help in such a powerful way?

Through years of praying about this, I have discerned that I simply needed it. Salvation is something no one can acquire on their own, and I was so desperately lost. I have come to understand that desperation is, in fact, a gift. (Mark 5:24-34 and Luke 8:42-48 articulate well the gift of desperation.)

I had been hearing in my head a voice telling me I was a worthless piece of junk, that no one could ever love me, that I was stupid and selfish and unworthy. I think years of abuse early on in my life had taken their toll. I was a victim of childhood sexual abuse, or CSA, and I had experienced abuse from the time I could remember until I was seven years old. I needed healing, and I needed forgiveness.

I needed to know who I was: a beloved child of God.

It was a cold spring morning in a home in Cleveland, Ohio, where I experienced God firsthand. I had read a lot about God, and I had heard God speak to me through the scriptures when I was younger, but this day was different. This day, I received supernatural healing and forgiveness. Even as I type this, I feel awkward about it. It sounds weird and it makes me embarrassed, but that is what happened to me. When Jesus saved me, he saved me spiritually and physically.

After this experience with God, I no longer wanted to take my life, and I wanted to live for God and not myself. I began reading and, for the first time ever, understanding the Bible. It was an exciting time in my life. I began to pray and ask God where he wanted me to live and how he wanted me to live.

I also began to read Corrie Ten Boom's book, *The Hiding Place*. There is a place in the book when the war is over and she is traveling around trying to help Germany heal. She speaks, and afterward the guard who imprisoned her and her sister and father in the concentration camp comes up to her. Of course she recognizes him, but he does not recognize her. He holds out his hand and thanks her for what she is doing for Germany.

Corrie prays in that moment and tells God: "I can't. I can't shake this man's hand. I cannot forgive him."

And she hears back. "I know, Corrie. You can't but I can. Now, hold out your hand."

And she shakes his hand.

I read this and lay down on the ground weeping, saying over and over, "I forgive you. I forgive you," to the man who abused me who died the previous year. For me, this was a path to freedom and the beginning of my healing. It was not the end. It was just the beginning.

Almost twenty years later in 2011, while in seminary at Fuller Theological Seminary, I would become painfully aware that I had not forgiven myself and others connected to my abuse. I call this time my "Good Friday period." I could also refer to this as three days in hell, but it was a lot longer than three days. I did a few things that were difficult but helped me heal even more.

First, I got professional help from a trusted Christian counselor who was trained in Eye Movement Desensitization and Reprocessing, or EMDR. This counseling helped me forgive myself and process as an adult what happened to me as a child. If you are a victim of trauma, I cannot recommend this enough. I just cannot say how important it is for people to seek professional help from trained mental health professionals who are also Christian.

Also, I finally told the whole truth to my family. It was horribly painful for my brother, but he did the most beautiful thing for me. He asked me if anyone had ever expressed how sorry they were that this happened. I wept as I turned off supper and proceeded to have a deeply meaningful conversation with my brother.

I think this has implications for us right now as a church. If you know someone who has been a victim of injustice or oppression or abuse, simply expressing to them how sorry you are will aid in their recovery process. My brother was not a part of the problem. Yet he chose to be a part of the solution. I will always be grateful to my brother for his empathy and compassion.

Fast forward to 2020. I was finally getting ordained. I had a church that I absolutely loved serving. Then CO-VID-19 hit! So many, many people were rightly concerned about the elderly and those with comorbidities and how many lives COVID would claim. But me, I was asking: How many young people's lives were claimed last year because of suicide? What is the number one or number two killer among people ages ten to twenty-one? While we had great responses to keep our elderly and those with physical comorbidities safe, what are we doing about the growing mental health problem among our young adults? How was COVID affecting their mental health? Where are we in response to this growing pandemic?

We currently have a Christian licensed professional counselor on our staff who meets the emotional needs of some in our church community as well as out in the larger community. This is something our church has decided to do in response to the growing number of people who are struggling with mental health issues.

Jesus ministered to the whole person. He met the physical, spiritual, and emotional needs of those he encountered. As I write, I am reminded that he first said to the paralytic, "Take heart, son; your sins are forgiven," before telling him, "Get up, take your mat and go home" (Matthew 9). I think this text speaks to us so clearly the importance of receiving and giving forgiveness.

So, church, I say to you: In the name of Jesus, you are forgiven. I pray that you would say back to me and others like me: And in the name of Jesus, you are forgiven.

May we care about the spiritual and emotional well-being of one another as much as we care about the physical wellbeing. Let's bring Christ, the balm of Gilead, to our communities and be places of forgiveness and healing for those who are suffering.

Sullivan is a pastor in South Carolina.

12

A Candid Conversation

By Erica Whitt

Early in the COVID-19 pandemic, the pastors at Bethel United Methodist Church in Spartanburg, South Carolina, began to create a plan for how to respond to what was sure to be a mental health crisis in response to the pandemic. They had insight that people interacting through Zoom meetings without face-to-face contact would quickly take a toll on the emotional wellbeing of our community.

They reached out, and we compiled a list of local therapists and nonprofits that could be shared with individuals in need. At this meeting, we discussed creating a plan to address big-picture mental wellness concepts with the youth in our church when we returned to regular in-person meetings.

In fall 2021, we started a seven-week group focused on growth mindset. Our curriculum was based on *Big Life Journal,* of which each participant received a copy. I led the group through the journal, and Chad Deetz, our youth minster, brought in the spiritual component that reinforced the concepts being presented. We felt this allowed youth the opportunity to see that mental health and spirituality can stand together to help us be happy and whole individuals.

We discussed forming new neural pathways for positive

thinking, setting goals, recognizing strengths, and seeking support in times of adversity. We also tried to normalize failure, letting our youth know that failure can be the greatest teacher of all and that there is a support system around them when they do mess up.

But following a week with multiple losses in the community, we went off-script from *Big Life Journal* to focus on two hard topics: death and suicide.

The entire mood of the group shifted that night.

Our youth went from typical teens, who would get distracted at times, to one hour of total attention and respect for anyone who shared. We discussed the importance of asking for help when you need it and appropriate ways to be there for your friends when they might need it. We talked about the value that every youth has no matter what they may be struggling with or feeling rejected about.

Older youth took on a leadership role and shared personal stories of struggling but also overcoming. The vulnerability displayed by those who shared allowed younger youth to better recognize that some of the people they look up to have gone through hard things, but they have also been able to overcome those challenges.

I know that the seeds planted and the stories shared that night will stick with our youth. I am hopeful it will allow them to not only support each other but also support friends outside of youth group as they face the challenges that come with middle and high school and into their adult years.

While the youth met, parents were invited to meet with Bethel's pastors, the Revs. Megan and Brad Gray. This integrative approach allowed the parents to know what the youth were being taught. The idea was this would allow them, when appropriate, to reinforce these skills.

Yet it was just as much to remind them that they don't have to save their children every time they struggle. Parents were able to explore coping skills to use in times of stress as well as work to identify the different strengths in each member of their family. Parents were able to process the struggles of parenting teens growing up with constant connection and discuss ways to set healthy boundaries.

Overall, the parents may have taken away as much as the youth and hopefully were able to remember that our church family can be one of our greatest supports.

Whitt is a member of Bethel United Methodist Church in Spartanburg, South Carolina.

13

In Spite of It, We Are Loved

By the Rev. Jamie McDowell

Mental health. It is a subject we often tend to ignore.

We tend to ignore it because it often carries us outside our comfort zone. We like to perceive ourselves as normal, well-adjusted people. Many times we claim to be saved by Christ, thus we cannot allow a chink or crack to be visible in the armor of God.

We tend to place the sword of sexuality behind our back. We lay down the shield of insanity. We place the helmet of delusion on the ground beside us. We try to stand in front of the stallion of schizophrenia as we boldly proclaim our knighthood as well as our sainthood to the world.

However, as Christians we must come to understand that much like the possessed man in Mark, Jesus loves us. He approached the Gadarene with love and compassion. Jesus did not reject but accepted him. In fact, by the time their encounter was over, the Gadarene was not only a friend, but a follower of Jesus. He wanted to travel with and share Jesus' message.

As we read and begin to understand the stories of those who have and do continue to battle against mental health issues, we, too, must see them from a biblical perspective. We must understand that mental issues often loom like Goliath as those who overcome sling forth the pebbles of hope. We, too, must respond as the army of Israel to help track down and ferret out the last of the Philistines' fanatics and fantasy from the minds and bodies of our army.

We must understand that with God all things are possible, while understanding that God relies on humanity to assist each other in the battle on evil.

McDowell is a licensed local pastor in the South Carolina Conference of The United Methodist Church.

14

New Directions:
A Counseling Ministry

By the Rev. Charles Wilbanks

In the spring of 2019, I was the pastor at Trinity and New Chapel United Methodist churches in Newberry, South Carolina. I had been there for less than a year. As I got to know the community, I became aware of a critical unmet need in Newberry and Newberry County. The availability of affordable mental health screening and treatment was sorely lacking.

This issue was particularly important to me. I have been a social worker and am a licensed mental health counselor. I know firsthand the devastating impact that untreated mental illness can have on an individual, a family, and a community. I also knew well that available and affordable mental health treatment was lacking almost everywhere.

I wondered what the church could do to begin to meet that need. The church has been called to be the hands of Christ in the world. Indeed, our mission is, in part, to exemplify God's command to love God and neighbor. It became apparent to me that responding to such a critical community need would be a way for Trinity, New Chapel, and other area churches to engage in our called mission.

The need for a mental health ministry became even more apparent to me as I continued to gain data on the area's need for available and affordable mental health care. It was clear that although the need for such care was critical across demographic populations, the need was most acute for the uninsured, underinsured, and poor. It is undoubtedly true that most communities in South Carolina face this need, but it is especially true in Newberry and Newberry County.

This felt need eventually gave rise to New Directions Counseling Ministry. As I thought about what the church could do to respond effectively to this need, I first began to speak with leaders of the churches I pastored and with community leaders in Newberry and Newberry County. In that process, I spoke with church lay leaders, church council members, and others at my churches, as well as clergy at other churches in the area. Although many had questions and some had doubts, I received strong support for the potential of this ministry. I then spoke with community leaders. Most importantly, I spoke with the mayor, the police chief, and the sheriff. They had a keen appreciation for the problem surrounding the lack of mental health treatment. They reinforced the need for the increased availability of affordable mental health services for the poor.

Finding adequate funding for the new ministry was more challenging. Three attempts to receive grants failed. However, we eventually received funding from Trinity UMC (which endorsed it as an official ministry of the church) and New Chapel UMC. Also, O'Neal Street UMC agreed to provide New Directions with needed space for a counseling center. In addition, Newberry Area Council on Ministries provided a generous donation to help us to launch New Directions.

The new ministry's envisioned purpose was to provide

affordable screening, assessment, mental health counseling, and referral services for persons struggling with a variety of difficult life issues and to offer opportunities for spiritual growth and wellness. The services the new ministry sought to address were depression, anxiety, stress management, bipolar disorder, couples counseling, and grief and loss.

The approach of New Directions was that we would attempt to expand existing treatment services for the uninsured and the poor. It was not aimed at duplicating existing community resources, which were few, but to create and to expand available mental health resources that were affordable to all. New Directions was not meant to respond to those in need of inpatient services or in need of hospitalization. Those clients would be referred to other service providers.

The space that was provided by O'Neal Street UMC, under the leadership of the Rev. Amanda Richardson, was conveniently located to most people who might need to take advantage of the facility. Trinity was not suitable since it is in a rural location some twenty minutes from downtown Newberry. The support and assistance of the Greenwood District Office, and the leadership of Dr. Stephen Love, was also critical in our effort to launch New Directions. The ministry was to begin with limited ability to staff a screening program. Because of that we sought and received an agreement from the Free Clinic of Newberry County to use their facility for the purpose of intake and assessment of those in need of the services that New Directions intended to provide. The Free Clinic was already equipped with staff and space to assist with that screening. The space at O'Neal Street was graciously refurbished for our use.

With some funding acquired, more than adequate space

identified, and screening capability secured, we were ready to launch the ministry in the early spring of 2020. We identified and looked forward to launching New Directions on March 23, 2020. In the days prior to March 23, we received several referrals and arranged appointment times for counseling at the O'Neal Street Counseling Center.

However, before March 23, the area was hit hard by the growing COVID-19 pandemic. After speaking with the leadership group, supporters, and referral sources, it was decided that to move forward with New Directions was unwise. Soon, the two major referral sources, the Free Clinic and Newberry County Memorial Hospital, had severely restricted operations because of the growing pandemic.

Unfortunately, New Directions had been shut down just as it had launched.

After a few weeks, however, the Free Clinic reopened with more restrictive guidelines and screening. While the counseling center remained closed, the Free Clinic generously agreed to provide space within their facility for counseling sessions. They also provided screening, assessment, and COVID safety checks for clients. So in a sense, New Directions was eventually launched later in the spring of 2020 within the Free Clinic. It was not what was envisioned as we had designed the ministry. Moreover, the pandemic made the implementation of this ministry extremely difficult. However, we were able to provide counseling services in a somewhat more modest way.

Because the counseling center at O'Neal Street was closed, our footprint in the community was reduced and our ministry was more hidden from the community. That, of course, was an obstacle to growing New Directions. However, we were able to serve the people we intended to serve (although less effectively and extensively).

It was disappointing that the potential for New Directions was diminished just as it was becoming functional.

The need that New Directions identified and had just begun to meet still exists, not only in Newberry but across the state in many different communities. The lack of available and affordable mental health treatment for the uninsured, underinsured, and the poor persists.

I remain convinced that the church has the opportunity, the resources, and the calling to address this critical need. I pray that, as a church, we will be able to do that.

Wilbanks is a retired elder in the South Carolina Conference of The United Methodist Church.

Suicide Warning Signs

The behaviors listed below may be some of the signs that someone is thinking about suicide.

Talking about:
- Wanting to die
- Great guilt or shame
- Being a burden to others

Feeling:
- Empty, hopeless, trapped, or having no reason to live
- Extremely sad, more anxious, agitated, or full of rage
- Unbearable emotional or physical pain

Changing behavior, such as:
- Making a plan or researching ways to die
- Withdrawing from friends, saying goodbye, giving away important items, or making a will
- Taking dangerous risks such as driving extremely fast
- Displaying extreme mood swings
- Eating or sleeping more or less
- Using drugs or alcohol more often

If these warning signs apply to you or someone you know, get help as soon as possible, particularly if the behavior is new or has increased recently.

If you're thinking about suicide, are worried about a friend or loved one, or would like emotional support, the Lifeline network is available 24/7 across the United States.

988 Suicide & Crisis Lifeline
Call or text 988
Chat at https://988lifeline.org/
Text "HELLO" to 741741

—From the National Institute of Mental Health

"And surely I am with you always,
to the very end of the age."
— Matthew 28:20

About the Editor

Jessica Brodie is an award-winning journalist, author, blogger, editor, writing coach, and devotional writer with thousands of articles to her name. Since 2010, she has served as the editor of the *South Carolina United Methodist Advocate*, the oldest newspaper in Methodism, which has won 123 journalism awards during her tenure. Learn more at https://www.jessicabrodie.com